Jesus

Rusty Barnes

Nixes Mate Books
Allston, Massachusetts

Copyright © 2017 Rusty Barnes

Book design by d'Entremont
Cover photo from the collection of Lauren Leja

All rights reserved. This book or any portion thereof may not be reproduced or used in any manner whatsoever without the express written permission of the publisher except for the use of brief quotations in a book review or scholarly journal.

Some of these poems appeared in *Chiron Review, Poets & Artists, Busted Dharma*, and *Pressure Press Presents*.

Thank you to Michael McInnis first, as well as Doug Holder, Al Maginnes, Joshua Michael Stewart for long-time support, and Gloria Mindock for her readings in the Červaná Barva space at the Armory in Somerville.

ISBN 978-0-9991882-7-9

Nixes Mate Books
POBox 1179
Allston, MA 02134
nixesmate.pub/books

For Heather Sullivan, the only woman ever

Contents

Annus horribilis	1
Feeding Beer to the Ducks at Night	2
Thunder Key	4
Dream Poem #3	6
Summer 1974	8
Listening to Hugo Winterhalter in the Early AM	10
The Water Eternal	13
Stalker	14
Sometimes I Say	16
Jesus in the Ghost Room Talks with the Father	19
The First Time	20
Fire	22
After Midnight	24
I Have a Reservation	26
Pissing Out a Fire	29
The Meteor as Explanation; A Poem of Witness	30
The Bush of Exhaustion	32
The Path of No Path: Breakheart Reservation	34
My Father's Hip: 1972 Flood	35
Arrow-Fishing	36
Circus	37

Country Bullshit Childhood	38
Poem for Another Poet	41
The Esplanade at Midnight, 1993	42
Free Fill	44
How You Died	46
Not Much Better Sober	47
Texas Will Kill You Back	50
The Suicide of Gnats	53
The Things that Happen in a Day	54
I Remember	55
The Damned Middle of the Store	56
The Things We Wish We Were	58
Tonight's the Night: April 10th 2016	60
Earthquake	62

Jesus in the Ghost Room

Annus horribilis

This is the year of terrible things,
the moss doesn't even grow on
the right side of the tree any more
along with all those other things some-
one told me. The milk runs up
the table leg back into the bowl
and the cereal into the box
I'm leaving your body the same
way the rush of wetness suddenly
dry. We are back at the picnic table
at midnight and my hands swirl in
the air on their way back to your pockets.

Feeding Beer to the Ducks at Night

You fill a hubcap with the cheap
bread you buy from the gas station

and soak it in cheaper beer.
Leave it by the abandoned

car hood which serves as shelter
for the animals, next to the pond.

Watch and giggle as the ducks
waddle uncertainly to the water,

their webbed feet tipping sideways
as they spraddle-leg and sway in

the loose moon-beamed dark,
your brothers lighting smokes

off silver Zippo lighters laughing
at the throaty quacking as the

animals nod off and I sit on
your tool-box admiring the man

I will probably become some day
soon when the ducks sober up

and everyone at this party
waits for the quotidian dawn.

Thunder Key

Sue says thunder is due and I am
the lightning bringing quick rain

and the inevitable tree fallen across
the power lines and phone lines

and the scruffy volunteer firemen
coming to the door and telling us

to go get out and the ocean spins
against the jetty like something alive

and someone is walking their dog
on the beach while lobster traps

burst open on the rocks like candy
from a wrapper and the surf is now

within a few feet of the running mutt
and I am the lightening of the sky

and the boredom on the TV screen
which brings nothing in but fuzz.

I am the interferon when no one else
is ill and I am the sick bastard

who doesn't care about this world
but instead the worlds I create.

I am not fit for children or family
and I am always way too fucking late.

Dream Poem #3

High on Tower Hill I walked down
what seemed to be a logging road
which petered out into a deer path.

At the end like a prize I found the head
of a girl child recently parted from its body
gore hanging from its neck (I can't use

the right pronoun here, I just can't) sway-
ing in the wind, its false body made of pieces
of metal, rattling and shaking. I knew

I had to take revenge so I followed
another trail through a river dark with fog
and the sounds of frogs echoing.

In front of me big as life a house boomed
like no noise I'd ever heard. I kicked
the door open and four small children

leapt from the shadows at once,
attacked with their teeth and claws.
Between them they had one frightening

face which they tossed to each other
sharp fangs bared and empty eyes
before they attached themselves

to my limbs to try to bring me down.
I woke to the real then, to the toe
I broke kicking the bedpost

in my sleep. Four children. One face.

Summer 1974

Sky red as sunburn,
the garden blooming lush.
I've been chucking rocks
out of it all day long, mom
digging out potatoes with
her bare hands. Dad comes
home from work hands
still greasy, cigarette packs
rolled into both sleeves like
epaulets. He picks up
the potato and tells me
to wash it off in the crick.
I do, and he cuts off half
and gives it to me with
a salt packet from Mickey D's.
He shakes the salt on the raw
potato and tells me to bite
into it like an apple. The sun
is just there through the trees
and the wind picks up a little
as it flutters through the garden
like a hummingbird. The taste

is dirt and a little bit of grease
and that wonderful salt which
now leaks out of my eyes.

Listening to Hugo Winterhalter in the Early AM

In Japan a gull carries away
a kite string as the moon breaks

into a silent but yawing sea,
a warning to me to you to us all:

O Father you have gone where
I cannot find nor follow you,

pliant in your yeast-smelling blanket
coughing up your identity with

every wrack and sough. I sit beside
you playing thirties jazz and pop on

my tablet tears slicking the screen.
You have gone behind the blue

curtain past the barrier strange past
the stinking offal in the suicide forest.

O father what could I have done
but be here tight on your heels tapping

my fingers to the sounds of Benny
Goodman for seven hours in the car

awaiting your death or my leaving
whichever comes first. O Father

I wish I could invoke your smell,
the way your cigarette ashed onto

The sick-filled carpet on the edge
of what we could readily say,

blinded right now to our faults,
both of us sighing together against

the sea and into a heavy head-wind
at the edge of nowhere and every time

we batten the hatches the sea comes
up and washes you away down

the nameless dreary paths of alphabet
and stone and, O Father, forever.

The Water Eternal

Some reasons I love you:
your Ouroboros tattoo,

the way your paired hipbones
slice their way from your jeans,

twin throttles of the engine
that drives your center,

and where else but in a poem
can I talk about the shape

of your neck as it curves into
your shoulder meeting at the mole

that makes a stunning target
for my lips. Your belly and root

heavy with breath/the soft flutter
of your navel,

the taste of cinnamon and orange
of your sex.

Stalker

My ear is pressed to your door
which is a thing a pervert or stalker
would do but I am just a boy
with his liver in his hands waiting
to give it to you because hearts
are just too cliched. Outside my
friend Billy revs the engine on
his fuckt up 1979 Bandit Trans Am.
He's not really a friend just a guy
from up the road who happens
to have a driver's license and a car
that isn't up on blocks so everybody
uses him to get places. My parents,
hell everybody in my family would kick
my ass if they saw who I was with
but I don't care because this girl is 19
and so unattainable to me at 13
that I have to try so I knock softly
and hope she'll come to the door
in leg warmers after jacking the volume
on her Journey tape but she's in
there with someone else and Billy

wants to go get pizza so I leave
her porch with my hardon
and dreams of her 80's bush.

Sometimes I Say

Sometimes I say to you suicide
and you say slice by length not

by width, and judge carefully
the angle of the blade

at the rise and tumble of the vein.
If you wanted bravery you should

have broken my fingers. I am bravest
choking on my own blood. The white

fish that swim in the burl of my body
seek shelter in the granite of my

lungs. When I say to you heart
I mean brain and when I say brain

I mean give me a razor or speed
enough to hustle my heart into

infarction. Let's not bedazzle it to ourselves on social media and complain

that no one pays attention. Everyone
is into their own slow suicide; the smart

ones among us simply hurry
the process. What we are after all

is the cause of our own deaths.
We tunnel after cures and burn

the pleasure from life with each detox
and every cleanse. I believe every

one deserves a dirty death. It's not
enough to howl into our hands

or fuck the grief to dust or die
alone in a garret apartment or

mobile home waiting for maggots
who will turn to flies. At least they love

our rot. Death means noise. Call
to Heaven-that-is-not-there.

Crack the wombs of statues,
cast your orgasms in granite.

Take the last mean words you
can muster--use them to trepan

your skull. That hole is important;
at the end of it all: let the sere light

in. Only then you'll be saved, if that
even matters to you after so long a trip.

Annihilation is not a punishment. No.
The ending is not a beginning of anything.

Jesus in the Ghost Room Talks with the Father

Jesus fills the cancer room with stuttering
ghosts. It's something about salvation;
if you don't achieve it you can never speak
afterward so all these spirits float around
and manifest themselves as balls of light
or knocking doors or the cold feeling you
get in a room empty of light and singing.
The people alive in the interferon glow of
chemo have much the same problem. They get
tired and go to sleep in their son's bedrooms
while the whirling stars of immanent chaos
warm their bodies with heat generated from
the nearby coppiced souls. Let's not kid
ourselves. The things you say here don't
matter a bit. God in his eminence gave you
Jesus to serve as middleman and it's been
two thousand years of terror and failure. The idea
of God – forgive me father – brings me only pain.

The First Time

I'd like to tell you about my first sex-
ual experience but this is not
that kind of poem. I sat in a tire
tube in the middle of the small
lake we called Packard's Puddle
with a half a sixer of beer
and my left middle finger doing
its holy work in the vagina
of a skinny girl I knew as Claire,
though I don't know if that was her
name because when I wrote her
letters the answers came back
signed by Karen. I recall every
second before we both discovered
the key to female orgasm and as I
feathered my other hand in the lake
to keep us from drifting in, the beer
floated outward and I stopped what
I was doing to grab it and Claire tipped
me over like garbage into a Dumpster.
It ended in the shallows as she rode
my hand to heaven and I cracked

my skull on a rock and pledged eternal love to a girl I'd never see again.

Fire

I've not much to say about fire,
not much more than will appear

in this short form. I remember
fire early on in my life. the way

the metal screen on the fireplace
popped with sparks like the flame

from the Zippo my father used to light
his Viceroys. I remember burning tires

in the barnyard to what purpose I
have no idea. I remember many

campfires like this one I pick as my
earliest memory: Left alone

as a toddler I saw the charcoal go
gray and thought it had gone out.

I picked it up and screamed. Burned
myself badly. Even now my left hand

is extra-sensitive to heat like many
of the memories I relate in these poems.

I remember them all as stages of hot
and cold and young and old and nervously

shaky, and whether or not I still
feel them as scars.

After Midnight

Somebody told me the lake
would light up at night like
underwater spirits After midnight
in the rocked off section of water
the snappers would rise and swim
to the shallow end where you
might catch them if you weren't
busy climbing your girlfriend's
thigh in the waist-high water
all covered by dark adult lust
the way she would grabble at
you in mid-orgasm the ministers
could only dream of and the old
man in the moon pervert stares
down the long miles of night
to catch you in the act in which no
one should be caught. Rise at
breakfast in the scent of sex
and smallmouth bass. Fry a fish
at nine ayem and begin again to
wait till night being careful not
to swallow a bone and to not forget

the gleam under her brown skin
in the hard light of dawn.

I Have a Reservation

I have a reservation at the turntable
where at any second I can listen to my
dad's Dixieland jazz scratching around

the insides of my head Al Hirt late
at night when the shadows bake my
brain better than the best pot ever did

or Jimmy Dorsey's orchestra or as Dad
got older the blues we could bond over
late at night when truth outs itself

in the things you refuse to say aloud
like what it means when Kenny Rogers
takes over your inner monologue

and proves that genuine country
is just a few tummy tucks and face
lifts away. The way we could talk

across the hall from my room to
his with Mom when she had long
succumbed to the sleep that dare

not speak its name in the house
that had no doors. We'd be up
till the middle AMs with my playing

Zeppelin's best blues or the acoustic
stuff I got into in college Robert Johnson
or Bukka White or Tommy Johnson we

could listen to it all like good friends
forgetting any arguments we had till
the morning when he would get up to work

a twelve hour day in the gravel pit
filling loader after loader like the mouths
at home he worked to feed and the in-

digent talents his youngest son got
from somewhere the kings of industry
forgot to sell to more responsible kids.

Finally we come to it. My dad is nearly 80
and he tells me there are lots of people
on the other side he hasn't seen in 60

years. He's looking forward to it,
and why shouldn't he? The neck
of my culpability in his death

is drawn daily. If only I had been,
what? I don't know, but the trees
feel tight when I walk in them

and they all whisper guilt
and in the background a scratchy
disc plays Come on in my kitchen.

it's not gonna rain outside
except in my head.

Pissing Out a Fire

I love dogs and cats and pissing out a fire,
the way the flames burn green for a moment

and then reduce to ash. Long live the resin-
filled pine and the twigs I use for tinder

and the way your body moves in the blanket
like a soft wind raising up from your sleeping bag

and falling away just as it reaches my face.

The Meteor as Explanation; A Poem of Witness

You see it was supernova late
in the evening and all the stars
big like bullets suspended in
the sky and you and me and us
on the hood of your Fairlane
in the strawberry fields beyond
the old orchard. Late dark
and the tick of the engine
cooling. Planes and the distant
cough of a backfiring car out
on the main drag miles from here.
Granville Center of exactly nothing
but I'm lost in the folds of a cute white
dress that seems to be all fabric.
While you are on top giving me
a hickey that would last for weeks
it seems like that sharp meteor might
have given me an idea or two but
witless wonder I slide my hands
up your stockings and my ring
lays a ripping gouge halfway down
your tight thighs and I slide up

into the heat of your groin. I smell
the sad scent of rose perfume
you pull me up to you and breathe
in my ear. Somewhere later that morning
I swear a bobcat screamed
and you froze in my arms like some
city girl. Your legs in my lap I drive
your car home, sleep in the backseat,
pick strawberries with you all day long.
We bring each other cold water at
the same time and I believe even
now that is love.

The Bush of Exhaustion

The death bush is what the kids
call it, a cranberry-red and thorny

beast taking over the front of our
home. My wife sends me out to clip

it and being of somewhat sound
body I sally forth with gloves

and gardening shears to battle
with its high crest and lengthy

arms only to emerge with thorn-
hurts along my trunk and arms.

Hayden Carruth's poem about
summer haying comes to mind,

and though I am no Christ figure
I feel the brunt of wounds brought

by simple work and think of my
father's dark-greased hands home

every night eventually to collapse
on the couch and sleep the dream

only exhaustion brings, and I love
him all the more for it, my father

of rage and fire and undeserved
kindnesses, and yes, I say this

now though he's dead, I remember
him best this way: exhausted, asleep.

The Path of No Path: Breakheart Reservation

I feel it most intensely here
in the twilight when the sun
trembles in the drops
of rain settling among
the conifers and maples,
when I remember him
coming home from work late,
lunchpail in one hand
hardhat in the other
and I am playing in the yard
running to him and catching
him by the dirty shirtsleeves
tied around his waist. The days
we spent wandering in woods
like these on no particular path
come back to me now,
tripping along hand-in-hand
with my father's ghost.

My Father's Hip: 1972 Flood

One day the crick rose a couple feet
after three days steady rain that brought
logs ramming into rocks and a couple
dead dogs floating in the brown spume.
My dad lifted me up and brought me
to the very edge of the eroded bank
that with every rainstorm came just
a little closer to our house. I don't recall
what he said to me but I felt safe next
to his gritty cheek and the typical cigarette.
Beside me my brother Joe jumped from foot
to foot excited as all hell to be a branch
in that raging water. He slipped down
the bank screaming but dad never lost
a beat still holding me he whipped around
and caught my brother by the back
of his shirt and horsed him up the bank
with one hand. He bitched my brother
out pretty heavily once he was safe
but sitting on his hip in the driving rain
I felt overcome by my smallness.
Like all kids I returned to the site
of the scene 30 years later, dipping my
young daughter's feet in that same water.

Arrow-Fishing

The pond has become marsh now
but when it was waist deep I would
go to the middle in the depths
of muck to arrow-fish for the huge gold-
fish my landlord had stocked years
before. I remember bringing the bow
to my eye and sighting like a gun
along the top of my thumb the string
tense in my fingers and the feeling
as if I were going under. I remember
overshooting as I adjusted my shot
for refraction. I didn't make that one
but eventually the hard heart of the world
won out and the goldfish became bones
on the bank killed by coon or mink.
But I love the tense thrill of the shot still
I have only to close my eyes to recall.

Circus

If the Ringling Brothers were alive today
they wouldn't know how to begin.

Freak shows today are everywhere,
if you know where to look,

there on the common field of life
with the tattooed and the pierced,

the extraordinarily hairy together
with the unfunny and the trolls

who try to ruin it for everyone who
is not so jaded. I can see the tents in

my mind, the huge spikes that serve
as pegs and the groups of rope fest-

ooned with elephant shit and stale popcorn.
It is pure magic and we only have so much.

Country Bullshit Childhood

*written after hearing off-mic news announcers make
fun of some people I could know. For Joe and Kim*

Raccoons in the backyard tipping over
the garbage like homeless fat men,

the dance of dandelion pollen
blowing over the hayfields,

riding a dirt road and killing
a woodchuck with a single shot

from a .22. Roaming the crabapple
orchard and making hand cannons

from soft lead pipe and firecrackers.
Jumping from the big beam into a pile

of hay. Shovelling out the drop. Getting
paid a dollar a day during haying season

working for a cheap-ass farmer. Having
your brother give you some of his pay

to make up for it. Sitting around a picnic
table playing euchre while the bats flit

and the bug zapper keeps its own time.
Swimming across the piss-warm water

of a farm pond at midnight. Showering off
the algae later on. Listening to the wind

rattle the plastic tacked over the broken
window. Riding a car hood dragged by

an ATV over the snowy fields at thirty miles
an hour. Playing paper dolls and listening

to Elvis or Donna Fargo's Funny Face
on the record player. Staying up till 4 AM

to watch the Olympic heavyweights fight:
Tyrell Biggs, Francisco Damiano, the great

Teofilo Stevenson who never fought because
of the boycott. Watching and wondering why

a family friend (name not given to protect
the guilty and well, weird) would pull a fake tittie

out of his pocket to show a 12-year-old. He
might have been drinking some of the elder-

berry and dandelion wine we kept in the cellar.
Stealing porn from wherever I could find it.

Learning the burn from Southern Comfort.
At 8 years old, dancing with my sister at

the Big Elm Fire Department hall at her
wedding. Hovering around the keg at my

brother's wedding several years later. Country bullshit
my ass. Some people live this life.

Poem for Another Poet

I wanted me some peppermint schnapps
(for the snowmelt, you understand) so
I ventured out into the ass-high drifts.
I know you drink nothing but cheap beer
so I have something to say that might
ease your troubled mind in the long night
of your conscience. Get you something
other than that swill you normally drink
like Jim Beam Rye or Templeton Rye
and sit down with your wife and pretend
you're in a Mexican bar and you've just
met or maybe go closer to reality and have
a coffee at that particular place and go back
out to your car and pour some of that rye
into your cup. Don't drive too far now,
but tell me later whether or not it was a good
idea. Buy something nice for the lady
and lay down your drunken self at the door
pray for Heraclitus and make sure you neck
that bottle of rye real good while you do.
He says you can't step in the same river
twice but I'd bet you a dollar or two that
he's wrong.

The Esplanade at Midnight, 1993

Standing on the bank of the river
Charles at midnight or so on a blue-dark

night as galloping runners trot by,
a woman laughs and the water echoes,

and I am in search of sex. I am
bored and lonely and it feels as if

this is the permanent primal state
of things — all balls, no blue chips —

and for this moment in time I am
the only straight man cruising here

on a Saturday night in the fall while
university undergrads puke in the trash

bins then freshen their breaths with
mints or peppermint schnapps.

My love is far away and I am a dread-
filled set of hormones in need of a kick.

I walk up Charles Street to the Sevens for
a drink then backtrack to the Harvard Gardens.

I meet the gaze of a woman with blue eyes
but shy away lost in my own loser-osity.

Tonight the huge crowd is college-aged.
The sound system plays Pearl Jam.

By this morning I will be yesterday's
news, a story in need of revision,

a brilliant orange ball of sunlight coming to
at dawn in the darkling womb of the Back Bay.

Free Fill

My father stood tall in his Dickies
and khakis, holding his hands

behind his back as if at rest when
I knew at once he would not rest

until I was through, his cigarette
twitching the ash from his fingers

like a reverse Ash Wednesday.
I was asking his boss for free fill

in order to build the baseball
field that served as my Eagle

Scout badge project. Every smirk
and smart remark the man had

ever made to him must have
kept him livid inside but still like

a proud man he kept his counsel
and I got my dirt. How it must

have galled him to let me do this
but it was important for me to see

the more than occasional pride
that must conflict with the love

one gives to a child that probably
doesn't deserve it but gets anyway.

How You Died

In the first 23 years of my life
I never had to say time to get
a gun because there were always

fifteen or twenty in the house
at any given time: hunting rifles,
shotguns, varmint guns, muzzle-

loaders, even a 1911A1 that
kicked like a crazy horse.
They're mostly in a different

house now and when I think
of suicide I never consider guns
because it'd leave a fucking mess.

I don't want to leave the world
more bloody than I came in. If
I have to leave body fluids

behind I know what I prefer.
I'll spit at Satan as he drags
me to hell where no one cares

how you died.

Not Much Better Sober

The stairs to the trailer were piled cinder
blocks with no rails. Difficult to climb
when drunk and not much better sober.

The concave floor just inside the door
grabbed at your shoes unsteady or not.

I want to make this poem of Uncle Mort's
cherry-flavored pipe tobacco combined
with the scent of my parents' bitter cigarette

smoke. How I collapsed my teenaged
body on the floor with a book or their color

TV, something we didn't have at our place.
stumbling into the cold house late at night
walking in hip deep snow to break the ice

in the dog dishes, how the dogs would
shuffle out with steaming breath and

straw on their coats. Their rough tongues.

Ode to the 19th Year

Sometimes I wish for being slim
and fit again, to have a reliable

power: my two arms and legs
against the world like a steely

Colossus or a great gorilla,
confident again that my muscles

will do their part under my skin,
to react in time when danger

arrives or to intimidate the ill-bred
from attacking me or mine, but

long-toothed age now halts
my step and hunches my gait.

At my last physical I measured
out not only my age but my virility.

Only six feet one inch makes me
average after a lifetime of being

taller and here the rub comes:
What is left for me after forty-six

years but a slow senescence or
an even steeper decline? How I

wish again to be young, straight
again the way I remember myself,

not this knock-toed and hammer-
headed me who must look to

the next stone before he jumps
across the stream without the

grace of the ground to catch him
in his leaping and so carefully

and instinctually to return him unhurt
to the dirt from which he came.

Texas Will Kill You Back

We drove a half-empty U-Haul from PA to TX
in three days, a hundred bucks in our pockets

and my wife's brand-new credit card. We
dragged a Pontiac 6000 with 230,000 miles on it.

In the cab of the truck we set a litter tray
made of a shoebox for the two cats who

rode with us, moving from lap to lap as they
saw fit but finding their best purchase and sun

on the dashboard with the empty soda cans
and a bottle of water that was not enough as

we drove through Texarkana and hit I-45
eventually, Conroe and Willis and small towns

galore before hitting the city and finding just how
massive and spreadout a place could be. We

salvaged furniture from two deeply closeted
men and found a store that would sell my wife

beads within seconds, it seemed. My wife got
a job she could work while in school, and I flustered

myself finishing my thesis for my graduate degree
and didn't find a job until Wanda at Barnes & Noble

took pity on me and hired me for $4.75 an hour.
I'd like to say I learned something from that but

no luck. I just got angrier and angrier at the rich
for being fortunate in ways I was not and angrier

at the many poor with whom I was competing
like roosters for jobs. Three streets over toward

downtown I found cockfights on Sundays and
turf wars between rival gangs evinced by the

bricks thrown through the 7-11's plate glass
windows periodically. We found an apartment

between the rich and poor sections, a nice place
and we've stayed between the rich and the poor

ever since. I feel good about that, not so much
about the homeless man shot 22 times the first

week of our living there, for having a silver gum
wrapper in his hands. Then I remembered: we're

in Texas; you kill someone, Texas will kill you back.
Those policemen doing the shooting, though?

I bet they're still alive.

The Suicide of Gnats

Hello, moon old friend.
A tree branch breaks against

The sky. I've tried so hard
To miss you since week's end.
Every day marks a slow step toward
The suicide of gnats who

Fly into my face as we sit under
The porchlight playing euchre
My dead old man
And a woman I've never seen who
Is eerily my mother. And how
The night is full of chance.

My dad says go for it all. Have
A bottle of rye on me. Deep, cleansing rain.

I watch him wash away into the clouds.
Goodnight, moon.

The Things that Happen in a Day

I drink dirty martinis six olives at a time.
Every cloud I see looks like a cloud.
At home the cats throw up in my shoe.

I throw up snake eyes.
Every situation I'm in is untenable.
At home my kids devour Proust and disown me.

Every woman I love looks like an unwinnable game.
In city bars leather bears hit on me.
In the country I can drink gallons of beer.

I listen to the music of water dripping.
In the country I can piss on any convenient weed.
In city bars my only gay friend rescues me.

At home the glass shatters when I break wind.
In city bars I wear a John Deere cap.
In the country I become obvious to myself.

I Remember

I remember the night Uncle
Ralph died. We all gathered
at the yellow house where
we kids played annie annie over.
I can still remember the smack
of the ball on the tin roof,
the big bushes by the side
of the house where the kids
playing had worn paths.
The adults sat inside the kitchen
drinking coffee and smoking
until the late hours. I remember
running my baby cousin JJ
all over the yard, him only in
his diaper and t-shirt, the dogs
barking all night and at the end
getting into the car listening
to the sound of peepers and
Aunt Evie's big throaty laugh.

The Damned Middle of the Store

I lean on my wife like a farting
oldster though I am only 46.
This delusional panting I'm doing,
this gauche goblin footstomp,
this sepulchral keening of hair
and hoof and thinly-veiled anger,
the pustulant rump of pain
in my heel is called plantar
fasciitis, and it is pissing me off.
We are in the yoghurt section
and I am now in the middle
of the slow cuddle of senility:
I am eating fucking yoghurt now,
I am willingly swilling sour milk
and having it come up all bile
and bitchiness, abrogation and intubation,
blathering and bollocks. I am old
before my time, the hobnails
in my heel like stepping on glass
and into dogshit all at the same time,
and we are barely into the cereal aisle.
God help me, where is the liquor,

where can I whip up a beddy-bye,
how can I hammer out another sullen
step without pissing myself in pain,
and where are the rewards duly
promised me as a person of integrity
and good sense? I must find another
reason for existence; it must be
here amidst the corn muffins or the
half-price roasted chickens mummified
in insulated body bags after their
life's time throttled in a cage with
overlarge breasts and stubbed feet.
I walk out of the stores leaning on her,
knock-kneed and nearsighted, limping
like Oedipus and his bummed foot,
my cane dangling like a curved rib
from the cage of this cart, my God, my God
is this what my old age has promised?

The Things We Wish We Were

The VFW on Bennington Street smells
of smoke and old people. We traipse in

every election year to duly cast our
ballots where we are met by cops

and elections officers but not many
voters. They seem to have better things

to do like blow dandelion clocks or
cram a sugar-crust pizza from Luigi's

into their pie-holes with little or no
concern with what's going on in

their city or their state. Sometimes I
make the mistake of caring about

the place I live. It would make me
feel so much better to sit on my sofa

to smoke a bone and quaff Cherry
Crush that I buy on sale at the store

but no. I thrust myself up and travel
out to be an example for my kids,

who are otherwise resigned to my
charmless hedonism and follow the good

example of their mother, a better human
than I could ever be. I am lazy like the fox

and cunning as the werewolf when it
comes to being a wastrel – I. Just. Don't

Care.

Tonight's the Night: April 10th 2016

I can remember my father
dealing the deck for euchre,

two then three cards
at a time, always scheming

for the quick game you could
finish on your lunch break.

He could look at you after
one hand and tell you all

the cards you were holding,
just before he'd set you.

Father, once I had the whole
deck in my hand,

but now I've been dealt three
nines and an attitude, the kind

of situation where I want to call
trump just to fuck with you

if only for the eyebrow you'd raise
at me once more and wink.

Earthquake

God is a liar. When an earthquake splits
the earth's skin in front of you

the only recourse is to move or to invoke
some long-forgotten hope in an afterlife.

Plate tectonics will dictate the length
and severity of your punishment,

that not-so-silent and hardly penitent
prayer to the saint protector Emygdius.

Successful or not you may as well
piss on your fingers and call it rain

for all the good it will do. Both root
and branch will tremble, we're told,

the very rocks break under the thundercrack
yet you will find no surcease in the after-

life. There are ways to die and then there
are ways. If the earth moves under your

feet don't write a song about it. Prepare
yourself for a permanent vacation where

skulls and bony points finger you to sleep,
where the moons are mere dust reflecting

fire so far over you your breath fails to
catch you can think of welcomes suitable

to your new home, not of fire and saltpeter
and the bare ends of sanity but a place

where every day your toes crack the surface
of earth and you fall forward only for forever.

About the Author

Rusty Barnes grew up in rural Appalachia but has lived in East Boston and Revere, MA for the past twenty years with his wife, poet Heather Sullivan, and their family. He's published his work in more than two hundred journals and anthologies. His poetry chapbooks include *Redneck Poems* and *Broke*, and his full-length poetry collection, *I Am Not Ariel*, appeared in 2013. His latest novel is *Knuckledragger*. *On Broad Sound*, Nixes Mate's first book, was published in 2016.

Nixes Mate Books features small-batch artisanal literature, created by writers that use all 26 letters of the alphabet and then some, honing their craft the time-honored way: one line at a time.

Other or Forthcoming Nixes Mate titles:

WE ARE PROCESSION, SEISMOGRAPH | Devon Balwit
ON BROAD SOUND | Rusty Barnes
HE WAS A GOOD FATHER | Mark Borczon
CAPP ROAD | Matt Borczon
THE WILLOW HOWL | Lisa Brognano
A WORLD WHERE | Paul Brookes
SHE NEEDS THAT EDGE | Paul Brookes
SQUALL LINE ON THE HORIZON | Pris Campbell
MY SOUTHERN CHILDHOOD | Pris Campbell
A FIRE WITHOUT LIGHT | Darren C. Demaree
LABOR | Lisa DeSiro
KINKY KEEPS THE HOUSE CLEAN | Mari Deweese
AIR & OTHER STORIES | Lauren Leja
HITCHHIKING BEATITUDES | Michael McInnis
SMOKEY OF THE MIGRAINES | Michael McInnis
THE LIVES OF ATOMS | Lee Okan
LUBBOCK ELECTRIC | Anne Elezabeth Pluto
STARLAND | Jessica Purdy
WAITING FOR AN ANSWER | Heather Sullivan
COMES TO THIS | Jeff Weddle
HEART OF THE BROKEN WORLD | Jeff Weddle
NIXES MATE REVIEW ANTHOLOGY 2016/17

nixesmate.pub/books

Made in the USA
Middletown, DE
20 November 2017